COUNTRIES OF THE WORLD

VIETNAM

EDWARD PARKER

Evans

TITLES IN THE COUNTRIES OF THE WORLD SERIES:
ARGENTINA • AUSTRALIA • BRAZIL • CANADA • CHINA
EGYPT • FRANCE • GERMANY • INDIA • ITALY • JAPAN
KENYA • MEXICO • NIGERIA • POLAND • UNITED KINGDOM
USA • VIETNAM

Published by Evans Brothers Limited
2A Portman Mansions
Chiltern Street
London W1U 6NR

VISIT OUR WEBSITE
Evans
www.evansbooks.co.uk

First published 2005
© copyright Evans Brothers 2005

Produced for Evans Brothers Limited by
Monkey Puzzle Media Limited
Gissing's Farm, Fressingfield
Suffolk IP21 5SH, UK

British Library Cataloguing in Publication Data
Parker, Edward
Vietnam. – (Countries of the world)
1.Vietnam – Juvenile literature
I.Title
959.7'044

ISBN 0 237 52754 5

Editor: Daniel Rogers
Designer: Mayer Media Ltd
Map artwork by Peter Bull
Charts and graph artwork by Encompass Graphics Ltd

Picture acknowledgements
All photographs were taken by Edward Parker apart
from the following, which were kindly supplied by:
Alamy 47 bottom (Jamie Marshall); Corbis 31 top
(David Butow); Eye Ubiquitous/Hutchison 51 top
(Isabella Tree); Mark Henley 45 top; Reuters 16 top;
Still Pictures 16 bottom (Jorgen Schytte), 34 bottom
(Jorgen Schytte), 38 bottom (Sean Sprague), 49 top
(Bios), 55 bottom (Sabine Vielmo).

Endpapers (front): An aerial view of Ho Chi
Minh City (formerly Saigon).
Title page: Vegetables on sale in Sapa
market in north-west Vietnam, close to the
Chinese border.
Imprint and Contents pages: A farmer herding
ducks through rice paddies near Cuc Phuong.
Endpapers (back): Young boys cycle past
harvested rice on the roadside in the north
of Vietnam.

The gold five-pointed star on the Vietnamese flag represents the unity of intellectuals, farmers, soldiers, workers and youths in establishing Communism in Vietnam, while the red background symbolises bloodshed and revolution.

A view over Hanoi City, the capital of Vietnam.

Vietnam is a densely populated country that enjoys a strategic position in South-east Asia. It is roughly the size of Italy or the state of New Mexico in the USA. To the north lies China, while to the west lie Cambodia and Laos, and to the east is the South China Sea.

THE SHAPE OF VIETNAM

On the map, Vietnam is shaped like the letter S. Many Vietnamese people also describe the country's shape as looking like a pole with a basket of rice on each end. The country is widest in the north and, south of the capital Hanoi, it narrows rapidly until it is just over 30km wide in the centre. South of the industrial city of Da Nang the country gradually broadens out again until south-west of Ho Chi Minh City the area is dominated by the huge delta of the Mekong River.

A DIVERSE COUNTRY

Vietnam is diverse in terms of its landscapes. It has rugged mountains, dense rainforest and a tropical coastline where golden, sandy beaches meet the deep blue waters of the South China Sea. Vietnam also has a very varied population, with more than 50 different ethnic groups. Its population has been influenced by the peoples and cultures of China, the Indian subcontinent and other neighbouring countries. Today, the population is a rich mixture of the descendants of

indigenous groups and various waves of settlers that came to the country during the last 4,000 years. In the more recent past, Vietnam was also heavily influenced by the French, who occupied the country for nearly 100 years between 1861 and 1954.

The Vietnamese people are proud of their country and their heritage that stretches back so far. However, Vietnam could also be considered a relatively new country, as the north and south sections of the country were only reunified in 1975. This was after the Vietnam War, which left hundreds of thousands of people dead and the country's economy ruined. Vietnam is still recovering from the effects of the war.

Vietnam is changing rapidly. In the last 10 years, new industries have been set up and Vietnam now has one of the fastest growing economies in the region. The new prosperity of the urban areas is encouraging people to migrate there from the countryside in search of better-paid jobs. At the same time, tourism has brought prosperity to some of the poorest regions of the country.

VIETNAM'S PROVINCES

CHINA

Sapa

Hanoi

Hai Phong

N

LAOS

Gulf
of
Tonkin

Vinh

Hue

Da Nang

CAMBODIA

Nha Trang

Dalat

Phan
Rang

Ho Chi Minh City Bien Hoa

Vung Tau

South China Sea

0   250km

0   150 miles

KEY DATA

Official Name:	The Socialist Republic of Vietnam
Area:	329,560km²
Population:	82,689,518 (2004 est.)
Official Language:	Vietnamese
Main Cities:	Ho Chi Minh City, Hanoi (capital), Hai Phong, Da Nang, Hue, Nha Trang
GDP Per Capita:	US$2,300*
Currency:	Dong (VND)
Exchange Rate:	US$1 = 15,786 dong £1 = 29,736 dong

*(2002) Calculated on Purchasing Power Parity basis
Sources: *CIA World Factbook, 2004*; World Bank; UN
Human Development Report, 2004

Despite Vietnam's bright economic future, there are still many challenges facing the country. The concentration of wealth and new jobs in urban areas is likely to increase the divide between rich and poor. Also, rapid economic development is often accompanied by environmental problems such as deforestation and air and water pollution.

A colourful market scene with produce grown in the Mekong Delta.

PROVINCES

1 Hanoi	23 Lai Chau	44 Binh Phuoc
2 Bac Ninh	24 Dien Bien	45 Lam Dong
3 Vin Phuc	25 Yen Bai	46 Tay Ninh
4 Ha Tay	26 Son La	47 Binh Duong
5 Hung Yen	27 Thanh Hoa	48 Dong Nai
6 Ha Nam	28 Nghe An	49 Binh Thuan
7 Hai Duong	29 Ha Tinh	50 Ho Chi Minh
8 Hai Phong	30 Quang Binh	51 Long An
9 Nam Dinh	31 Quang Tri	52 Ba Ria-
10 Thai Binh	32 Thua Thien-	Vung Tau
11 Ninh Binh	Hue	53 An Giang
12 Hoa Binh	33 Da Nang	54 Dong Thap
13 Phu Tho	34 Quang Nam	55 Tien Giang
14 Thai Nguyen	35 Quang Ngai	56 Kien Giang
15 Bac Giang	36 Kon Tum	57 Can Tho
16 Quang Ninh	37 Binh Dinh	58 Vinh Long
17 Lang Son	38 Gia Lai	59 Ben Tre
18 Bac Kan	39 Phu Yen	60 Hau Giang
19 Cao Bang	40 Dak Lak	61 Tra Vinh
20 Tuyen Quang	41 Khanh Hoa	62 Soc Trang
21 Ha Giang	42 Dak Nong	63 Bac Lieu
22 Lao Cai	43 Ninh Thuan	64 Ca Mau

Fan Si Pan Mountain is the highest in Vietnam and is often covered in cloud.

Vietnam's varied landscapes include high volcanoes (mostly extinct) and mountains, tropical beaches, wild rainforests and vast, fertile deltas. Although Vietnam lies entirely within the tropics, the wide range of altitudes, latitudes and weather patterns gives the country an extremely varied climate. Within Vietnam there are cool plateaux, regions of high rainfall and hot, arid coastal zones.

THE HIGHLANDS

Three-quarters of the country is mountainous. There are two main mountain ranges – the Hoang Lien and the Troung Son. The Hoang Lien range is located in the far north, close to the Chinese border, in the most rugged and remote part of Vietnam. It has many high peaks including Vietnam's highest mountain, Fan Si Pan Mountain, which rises to 3,143m above sea level.

The Truong Son mountain range (also known as the Annamite Cordillera) forms the Central Highlands which run almost the entire length of Vietnam, along the country's border with Laos and Cambodia. These mountains are less rugged than those in the north, and the cool forested highlands are home to the majority of Vietnam's minority ethnic groups and rare and endangered animals.

For thousands of years the highlands have been a barrier between Vietnam and its neighbours. Even today, the rugged terrain of both mountain ranges means that there are few roads. As a result, many of Vietnam's hill tribes have retained a traditional life of subsistence agriculture. Only in the fertile plateau areas, such as around Dalat, is there much plantation agriculture and high rural population densities.

A view of the fertile agricultural land of the Dalat Plateau.

Most of Vietnam's mountain ranges consist of limestone but there are also some granite formations, such as the highlands inland from the port of Nha Trang. In the central highlands erosion of the volcanic peaks has given rise to extremely fertile red volcanic soils.

LANDSCAPE FEATURES

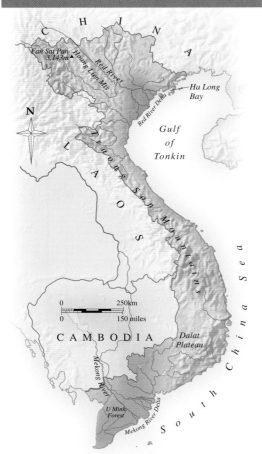

THE KARST FORMATIONS OF HA LONG BAY

The most striking of Vietnam's geological features are the karst limestone formations in the north of the country, especially around Ha Long Bay. Karst formations are created over thousands of years as water erodes and dissolves the limestone creating fissures, sinkholes and caves through which underground rivers often flow.

Ha Long Bay covers more than 1,500km^2 in the Gulf of Tonkin in north-east Vietnam. Here an enormous limestone plateau gradually sank into the sea over hundreds of thousands of years, leaving only the eroded peaks of the limestone mountains visible above the water. There are more than 3,000 peaks rising from the bay like giant teeth. In 1994 the area was designated a World Heritage Site because of its remarkable natural beauty.

Ha Long in Vietnamese, means 'where the dragon descends into the sea'. There is a local legend that tells how the bay was made by a giant dragon, which created the deep valleys as it ran from the mountains to the sea flailing its gigantic tail. The valleys were then inundated with sea water leaving just the peaks visible.

Some of the karst formations in Ha Long Bay.

THE DELTAS

The deltas of the Red River and the Mekong are two of Vietnam's major geographical features. The north-east of the country is dominated by the Red River basin, which contains the Red River Delta, a vast fertile region that is the main rice-growing area of the north. In the south, the Mekong River has produced one of the world's great deltas. Both of these delta areas are highly fertile and very densely populated.

The Mekong River originates in the Tibetan Plateau and flows over 4,500km to the South China Sea. Over millions of years, it has carried its load of fine silt eroded from the mountains upstream. This silt has been carried along by the swift-flowing waters of the Mekong and then deposited as the river slows down on the flat coastal plain in southern Vietnam. The result is a vast, flat area of fertile land divided by nine main waterways and thousands of shallow canals. The volume of silt brought down every year is so huge that the delta extends out to sea by an extra 50m to 100m a year. The water flow in the Mekong varies with the seasons. For example, in September the flow is a massive $38,000m^3$ per second while in May it is only $1,900m^3$ per second.

THE COASTAL STRIP

The coastal strip of Vietnam extends from the border with Cambodia in the south to the Chinese border in the north. The coastline is more than 3,450km long and is dotted with numerous small fishing villages and the occasional large city, like Da Nang. The central coastal strip runs between the Red and Mekong deltas and contains some of Vietnam's most arid landscape. Between just north of the port of Qui Nhon and about 150km south of Nha Trang, the climate is very dry and the landscape sandy.

Homes in the Mekong Delta are typically built on stilts.

There are many natural harbours along the narrow coastal strip of Vietnam.

In the far south-west of Vietnam is the U Minh Forest, which is the largest area of mangrove forest in Asia. Covering more than 40,000 hectares, it is home to many rare species including the red-necked crane, painted stork and spotted eagle. It comprises a mosaic of forest, grasslands and extensive peat swamps, which provide ideal conditions for crocodiles and many species of snake.

The forest was seriously damaged during the Vietnam War when US forces sprayed toxic chemicals to kill the trees, which provided cover for North Vietnamese guerrilla fighters. The chemical sprays, known as Agent Orange, not only killed the trees but poisoned the wildlife as well. Since 1975, most of the chemicals have broken down and become harmless, and the forest has regenerated.

In 2002, serious fires caused damage to 4,000 hectares of forest, though, once again, it is recovering. As part of the Vietnamese government's work to protect the forest, the U Minh National Park has been established, covering over 9,400 hectares.

Unlike most areas of Vietnam, where water is in plentiful supply, this part of the coastal strip is not good for agriculture. However, by using irrigation, crops such as mangoes, grapes and rice can be grown.

Vietnam has a wide continental shelf extending into the South China Sea. The shallow tropical waters above it are very rich in marine life and support large coral reefs.

The coastal region near the city of Phan Rang is the driest region in Vietnam. It has scrubby vegetation and a large system of dunes.

CLIMATE

Vietnam lies in the East Asian monsoon belt, and the general weather pattern is determined by two monsoons. The winter monsoon arrives from the north-east between October and March. The summer monsoon arrives from the south-west in April or May and lasts through to October.

However, within this general pattern, the climate varies greatly from place to place. This is partly because of the range of latitudes the country spans, from about 8° North to 23° North, and partly because of variations in altitude. Generally, though, the country can be divided into two broad climate areas – the north and the south.

THE NORTH

The climate in the north (roughly from Vinh northwards) is more extreme than in the rest of the country. There are two distinct seasons: winter and summer. In winter, which lasts from November to April, the north-easterly monsoon winds blowing from southern China bring cold weather to all areas north of Nha Trang. In the mountains, the temperature can drop to below freezing, and even in the Red River Delta it can fall to 8°C. Winters are not very wet, but February and March are marked by a seemingly unending drizzle, which the Vietnamese call *crachin*, meaning 'rain dust'.

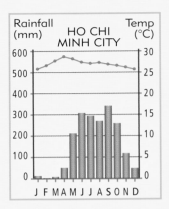

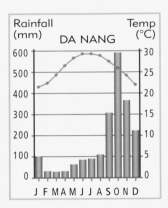

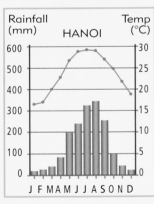

KEY:

Temperature   Rainfall

LEFT: A hot summer's day on the tropical coastline near Tuy Hoa.

Between May and October, moisture-laden summer monsoon winds blow in from the south-west, across the Indian Ocean and the Gulf of Thailand, bringing hot, wet weather to most of the north. Only areas sheltered by the mountains, such as the central Coastal Lowlands and the Red River Delta, avoid high rainfall. The northern summer can be extremely hot: in some areas the temperature can average 30°C. During the summer months, the north can be hit by severe storms known as typhoons (see case study).

THE SOUTH

The south of Vietnam (roughly south of Phan Rang) is tropical and stays hot all year round – between 25 and 30°C – though not as hot as the hottest months in the north. There are two main seasons – the wet and the dry. The wet season lasts from May to October or November. Ho Chi Minh City receives nearly 2,000mm of rain each year, most of which falls between the months of May and October. June, July and August are the wettest months in the south but even then the rain does not fall all the time.

The dry season runs from December to April, and includes the winter monsoon months when winds from the north-east bring hot, dry weather. The hottest months are March, April and May, when temperatures can rise to over 30°C.

CENTRAL VIETNAM

The climate of central Vietnam, roughly between the latitudes of 11° North and 19° North, is a mixture of those in the north and the south. The Coastal Lowlands in this region are sheltered from the wet summer monsoon by the Truong Son mountains. Most of the rain that does fall there arrives with the winter monsoon between December and February.

Inland, in the Central Highlands, the climate is temperate because most of the area is higher than 1,500m. This is the wettest part of Vietnam and it can have more than 3,300mm of rain a year, mostly during the summer.

The rainforests of the Central Highlands have very high rainfall.

Women workers filling baskets with coal at Coc Sau open-cast mine in north-east Vietnam.

Vietnam has numerous valuable natural resources, most of which have not been heavily exploited. It has large reserves of fossil fuels, such as coal, oil and gas, as well as reserves of valuable industrial metal ores including iron and bauxite (from which aluminium is produced). There are also deposits of precious metals, such as gold, and other useful raw materials including fine clay and limestone.

Vietnam has access to major marine resources in the South China Sea and has abundant water throughout 90 per cent of the country, sufficient to supply the needs of industry, agriculture and domestic use. There are more than 9 million hectares of natural forests in the country, which provide timber and fuelwood to rural populations. These forests also contain many different types of medicinal plants and other useful resources, such as rattan (used for canes and wicker), mushrooms and wild fruit.

Millions of people in Vietnam, particularly those living in rural areas, use wood for cooking.

About 50km north of the large coastal city of Nha Trang is one of Vietnam's main salt-producing areas. Sea water is fed, via a series of channels and dams, into shallow pools whose walls are only a few centimetres tall. The sea water is left in these shallow pools over a number of weeks until the water has evaporated leaving brilliant white salt crystals. The salt is then collected by hand and taken away for sale in local fish markets and beyond. Most of the workers are women, earning a wage of just US$3 per day. The work is very hard and the salt causes the skin on the

Workers carry baskets of salt produced by evaporating sea water.

workers' hands to dry and crack. Even so, US$3 per day is more than the average wage for this type of manual work in Vietnam.

METALS AND MINERALS

Vietnam is rich in both industrial metals and precious metals, which are used in the production of many products, from iron and steel used in shipbuilding to gold and titanium used in the electrical components in computers and cell phones. Other metals include copper, lead, zinc, manganese, bauxite and chromium.

The known reserves of these metals are mostly located in the north-east and central regions of the country. However, three-quarters of Vietnam consists of rugged highlands, which have poor roads and railways. It it thought that the remote north-west region of the country may have major reserves of metal ores.

In addition, Vietnam has significant deposits of useful minerals including fine china clay, which is used for making porcelain, and precious stones for making jewellery. Vietnam also has many of the minerals needed to support a growing construction industry, such as sand and quartz for glass manufacture and limestone for use in cement. The long coastline also yields useful products such as salt, made by evaporating sea water, and phosphates, which are used in the manufacture of fertilisers.

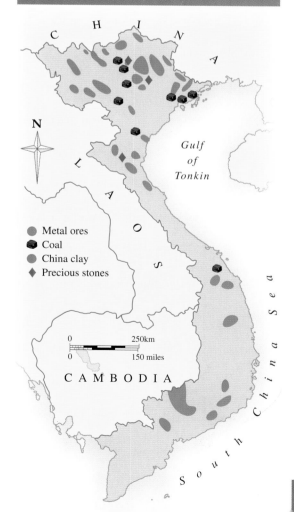

METALS AND MINERALS

- Metal ores
- Coal
- China clay
- Precious stones

0   250km
0   150 miles

ENERGY

Unlike many other developing nations, Vietnam is rich in energy resources. The provision of cheap energy is important for developing nations as new industries are developed and the demand for both industrial and domestic energy increases. Vietnam's energy is generated from three main sources: the burning of fossil fuels such as coal, oil and natural gas; hydroelectric power (HEP); and biomass sources, such as wood, rice husks and dung.

OIL, GAS AND COAL

Vietnam has large deposits of oil in six main oil fields, the most important of which are located offshore in the Cuu Long and Nam Con Son basins. Vietnam has at least 600 billion barrels of proven oil reserves, and further discoveries are expected in the next few years.

Associated with the major oil reserves are equally large reserves of natural gas. The use of natural gas in Vietnam is rising rapidly and a number of pipelines are scheduled for construction to bring this valuable resource onshore. In areas that are too distant from existing gas pipelines, the gas is lost when it is flared (burnt) off at the oil platforms.

Vietnam is fortunate in having huge reserves of high-quality anthracite coal. The estimated coal reserves in Vietnam are 147 million tons, most of which is high-grade. Most mines and coal deposits are located in the north-east of the country, particularly near Ha Long city.

HEP

The demand for electricity in Vietnam is rising rapidly. Presently, the numerous HEP stations around the country, including the Tri An plant near Dalat and the Hoa Binh station near Hanoi, produce more than half Vietnam's electricity. There are also huge amounts of untapped HEP available. However, while rainfall is predicted to remain at sufficiently high levels in the future, the destruction of forests in the catchment areas (see page 52)

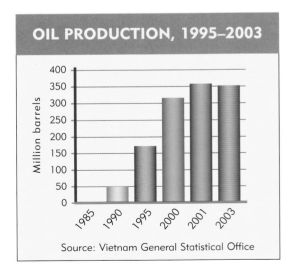

OIL PRODUCTION, 1995–2003

Million barrels (y-axis: 0, 50, 100, 150, 200, 250, 300, 350, 400)

x-axis: 1985, 1990, 1995, 2000, 2001, 2003

Source: Vietnam General Statistical Office

LEFT: Oil rigs are used off the coast of Vietnam to drill for oil.

LEFT: The Hoa Binh HEP plant, temporarily without water, provides electricity for Hanoi.

may lead to a reduction in generating capacity in the future. This is because the mountain forests regulate the flow of the rivers by absorbing water from the heavy seasonal rains and releasing it gradually throughout the year. Without the forests, the incidence of flash flooding and seasonally dry rivers will increase. In addition, soil from the deforested slopes is easily washed away, leading to the silting up of the rivers and the clogging of the HEP generating turbines.

ELECTRICITY GENERATION BY SOURCE (2001)

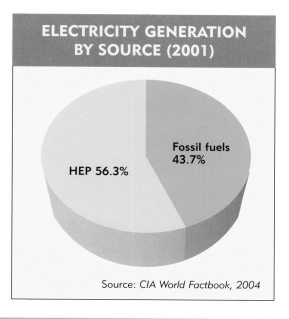

Fossil fuels 43.7%

HEP 56.3%

Source: *CIA World Factbook, 2004*

BIOMASS FUEL

Biomass fuel is any natural product, such as wood or rice husks, that can be burnt to make energy. In Vietnam, millions of people live in rural areas where there is little or no access to electricity or fuels such as coal and oil. These people typically use wood from natural and plantation forests for cooking and heating. Vietnamese farmers are generally very efficient in the way they use resources, and little is wasted. In many areas, the waste from agricultural products – such as rice husks and coconut shells – are used for fuel. Even dried dung from farm animals provides an energy source. The use of timber and other natural materials is a traditional part of Vietnamese life. However, the rapidly growing population and the destruction of the natural forests to

A man chopping firewood in a rural village near Sapa in north-west Vietnam.

make way for agriculture means that these resources will decline in importance over the coming decades.

FOREST PRODUCTS

Vietnam's natural forests comprise a patchwork of pine, broadleaf subtropical forest and lowland tropical rainforest, such as mangroves. These forests supply timber and other products including medicinal plants, wild fruit, honey, mushrooms and wild meat, such as deer and wild pig. However the use of forest products for construction, fuel and industry is leading to serious deforestation. Forests are also being cleared for agricultural plantations.

FISHERIES

The long coastline of Vietnam gives it access to some of the most productive fisheries in Asia. Fish is an important part of the Vietnamese diet, and thousands of fishing boats head out to sea every day to catch a wide variety of fish and shellfish. These include rays, cuttlefish, tuna, sardine, eels shrimps and shark.

The fish stocks of the South China Sea are under threat from overfishing, as fishing fleets from China, Indonesia, Malaysia and many other nations are drawn to the area. Lack of regulation on fish catches by neighbouring countries and disputes over territorial waters mean that catches are set to decline in the future.

ABOVE: Loading logs on to a truck in the Central Highlands.

BELOW: Landing fish at the large fishing port of Nha Trang.

WATER

The country has abundant water resources but they are not distributed evenly (the main dry areas are located in the narrow central coastal region). Water is particularly important to Vietnam, not only because of the country's large population but also because its staple crop is rice, which requires large amounts of water to grow. Although there are varieties of rice that can grow well without being submerged in water for several months, they are generally not as productive as the varieties grown in the deltas.

OTHER RESOURCES

Vietnam has a number of natural resources whose value is difficult to quantify precisely. For example, the country's stunning landscapes help to attract millions of tourists every year, earning millions of dollars.

Vietnam is also home to some of the world's rarest animals and has a remarkable, yet largely unrecorded, biodiversity. Among the large variety of plant species found in Vietnam are wild relatives of common farm crops and medicinal plants that could be very valuable to the future of agriculture or medicine.

An area of temperate forest in the Central Highlands near Dalat.

CASE STUDY
MANAGING THE FORESTS

In the highland forests inland from the city of Vinh, there are some very valuable types of timber, including yellow balau and keruing, which are used to make garden furniture for the US and European markets. In one area, the forest is being managed and harvested in a way that is close to being truly sustainable. The idea is to cut down only a limited number of trees per hectare and to cause as little damage as possible. Most community timber in Vietnam is harvested by hand. The loggers generally use large two-man handsaws instead of chainsaws, which means that the timber can be extracted with little damage to the surrounding trees. In this way the local community can extract timber for many years and foreign buyers will often pay more money for timber harvested in the least damaging way.

A woman rides her bicycle through a typical market in the Central Highlands.

The earliest evidence of humans in the area now known as Vietnam dates back to between 300,000 to 500,000 years ago, and the first appearance of settled agriculture can be traced back to 9,000 years ago. From 4,000 years ago, the Viet tribe – the ancestors of most of today's Vietnamese people – were engaged in struggles with various hill tribes and empires, and they eventually went on to conquer most of the country.

CHINESE AND EUROPEAN DOMINATION

Vietnam has been hugely influenced by China, its northern neighbour. Between 200 BC and AD 963, the Chinese and their way of life dominated the northern half of the country, introducing new agricultural techniques, systems of education and religion. South and central Vietnam escaped Chinese domination and were instead heavily influenced by Indian civilisation, introduced by sea traders and the neighbouring Khmer people to the west.

Between 1427 and 1789 Vietnam entered the golden age of Vietnamese dynasties after evicting the ruling Chinese Ming dynasty. Since the sixteenth century, Vietnam has also been exposed to European influence. The first Europeans to arrive were Portuguese traders. Then, in 1861, Vietnam became a French colony. Until then, the country had largely operated as a number of autonomous regions but the French effectively unified it. Vietnam finally gained independence from France in 1954. However, the French influence can still

be seen in some of the architecture in Vietnam, in the Catholic religion practised by some Vietnamese, and in the country's laws.

The opera house in Hanoi is a reminder of French colonial times.

THE VIETNAM WAR

Between 1946 and 1989, Vietnam suffered almost continuously from warfare, either on its own soil or, from 1978 to 1989, in neighbouring Cambodia. From 1946 to 1954, a war was waged against the French who had occupied Vietnam for more than 80 years. This led to the French being driven out and resulted in the country being divided in two. Communist North Vietnam was strongly supported by China and the former Soviet Union, while South Vietnam was backed by the USA. From 1964, the USA sent troops to support the South Vietnamese government against guerrillas operating in the south who were backed by North Vietnam. The conflict escalated into a war that eventually ended in 1975, when the North defeated the South and the whole of Vietnam became a Communist state.

The Vietnam War had major impacts on Vietnam's people, environment and economy, and they are still evident today. For example, in the decade from 1965 to 1975, it is estimated that between 800,000 and 1.2 million Vietnamese people lost their lives. About 10 million hectares of cultivated land and 5 million hectares of forest are thought to have been damaged in the same period.

An old man wearing his war medals in northern Vietnam.

23

The capital, Hanoi, is almost entirely populated by ethnic Vietnamese like this barber and his customer.

THE VIETNAMESE TODAY

Vietnam has 54 officially recognised ethnic groups, though the population is generally divided into three broad groups: the ethnic Vietnamese, the ethnic Chinese and the minority ethnic groups that make up the other 52.

ETHNIC VIETNAMESE

By far the largest of the 54 groups are the ethnic Vietnamese, who are also known as Kinh or 'people of the capital'. This group accounts for about 86 per cent of the entire population. The ethnic Vietnamese developed as a distinct ethnic group between 200 BC and AD 200 and since then they have supported themselves by growing rice. As a result, they have mainly settled in the lowland areas that are suitable for rice cultivation. Today they dominate the lowlands – the river deltas, the Coastal Lowlands and the large cities. They are also starting to influence the highlands more and more. Tens of thousands of lowland people have been resettled in highland areas that were formerly inhabited only by members of Vietnam's minority ethnic groups.

Vietnamese people who have migrated abroad are known as Viet Kieu, or overseas Vietnamese. Until the mid-1990s, Viet Kieu who returned to Vietnam were often treated poorly, being considered pampered, rich and arrogant by local people – though some of this ill-feeling may have been the result of envy.

ETHNIC CHINESE

The ethnic Chinese, or Hao, as they are also known, form a large economically important ethnic group of about 900,000 people. Originally, their ancestors migrated south from China into Vietnam because it was on an important trade route between India and China. They later settled close to Ho Chi Minh City, where they formed a large trading community. They tried to maintain their own Chinese identities, languages and school systems, and organised themselves into communities, known as *bang*, according to the province in China from which their ancestors came and the dialect they spoke.

Today the ethnic Chinese are still mainly concentrated in the south, and especially in the Cholon district of Ho Chi Minh City. Many of them have intermarried with the ethnic Vietnamese but there are still some groups who maintain a largely traditional Chinese lifestyle and continue to speak Chinese languages.

The ethnic Chinese are well known for their business sense, and prior to the fall of South Vietnam in 1975 they were estimated to have controlled around half of all the economic activity in the country. In 1978 the ruling

An ethnic Chinese shop in Cholon Market, Ho Chi Minh City.

ETHNIC ORIGINS

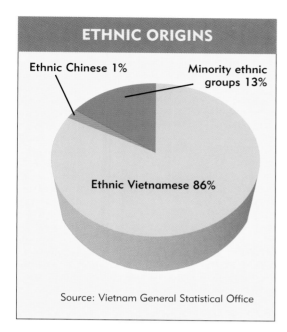

Ethnic Chinese 1%

Minority ethnic groups 13%

Ethnic Vietnamese 86%

Source: Vietnam General Statistical Office

meaning 'mountain people', and today they are still often referred to as hill tribes. Many share close ties with groups living in nearby countries such as China, Laos, Cambodia, Thailand and Myanmar (Burma).

CASE STUDY
THE HMONG

The Hmong migrated into Vietnam from China in the nineteenth century. Today they are a very large group and live scattered across the rugged north-west of the country. In 1999 their population stood at just over 797,000. They are considered to be among the most underprivileged of all Vietnamese people.

Typically, they live at high altitudes and cultivate rice, fruit and vegetables. There are several groups within the Hmong, including Black, White, Red, Green and Flower Hmong, each wearing a slightly different version of the traditional dress. The Black Hmong are very distinctive with their indigo-dyed blue clothing.

Black Hmong women selling blankets near Sapa.

Communist Party launched a campaign against the wealthy Chinese population, persecuting many for accumulating wealth. In 1979 China retaliated by attacking Vietnam and eventually about a third of all Chinese people fled the country for the safety of China and other countries, including the USA, Australia and France. Many Vietnamese officials now recognise that this anti-Chinese campaign was a tragic mistake that affected the economy very badly.

MINORITY ETHNIC GROUPS

Vietnam has one of the most diverse and complex ethnic populations of any Asian country. Members of Vietnam's minority ethnic groups (excluding the ethnic Chinese) constitute slightly less than 13 per cent of the total population. Many of these groups are quite small: 36 of them have populations of less than 100,000, and the O Du number only about 300 people. The Tay (with 1.5 million people), the Thai (1.3 million) and the Muong (1.1 million) are the largest groups.

All but four of the minority ethnic groups live in the highlands. Because of this, the French referred to them as *montagnards*,

POPULATION GROWTH

Vietnam's population has grown from 13 million at the beginning of the nineteenth century to over 82 million in 2004. However, this growth has been far from constant. In 1945, for example, the population fell by more than 2 million (from 22 million to 20 million) after the country suffered a terrible famine. Wars have also led to decreases in the population and at the height of the Vietnam War, from 1965 to 1975, between 800,000 and 1.2 million people lost their lives. During and after the war, up to 2 million people fled the country as refugees.

Today, Vietnam's population is increasing by 1.4 per cent per year. Again, the recent increases in the population have been far from even. After the Vietnam War, the Communist government organised a pro-birth campaign in order to help replace the human losses of the conflict. As a result the population increased dramatically. More recently, Vietnam's government has encouraged family planning to try to limit the growth of the country's population.

Motorcycles, cars and vans in a densely populated area of Hanoi.

While the urban population growth has been significant in the last 30 years, the population growth in the rural uplands has been even more dramatic. In 1900 the Central Highlands population was about 240,000. By 1960 this had risen to 600,000 and by 1976 it had reached 1,226,000. The population almost doubled again between 1976 and 1985 to 2,013,000. In the last 15 years the population has doubled once more and now stands at over 4 million.

POPULATION, 1950–2050

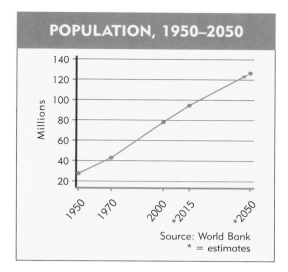

Source: World Bank
* = estimates

POPULATION STRUCTURE, 2004

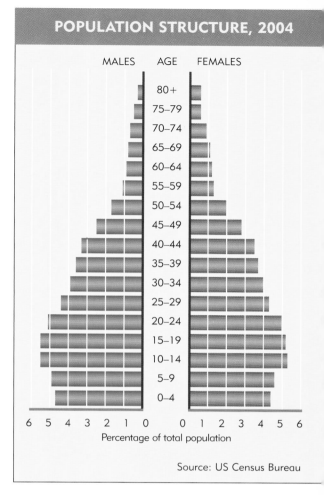

Source: US Census Bureau

POPULATION STRUCTURE

The structure of Vietnam's population is unusual, partly because of the effects of the Vietnam War. Because of war deaths, mostly among men, every population age band over 30 contains significantly more women than men (see graph on right).

Another factor is the government's post-war pro-birth campaign (see page 26). Although it ended in the mid-1990s, it still affects the country's population structure. As a consequence of the high birth rates since 1975, Vietnam has a very young population, with almost 60 per cent under 30 years of age. This is causing major problems in the provision of education and employment.

A father proudly holds up his young daughter in My Tho, southern Vietnam.

POPULATION DISTRIBUTION

Vietnam's population is unevenly distributed throughout the country. The population is very concentrated in the Red River and Mekong deltas, where densities of more than 1,000 people per square kilometre are not uncommon.

Population densities in the highlands are much lower than in the delta areas, but the highlands are less able to support a high population than the intensively farmed lowlands. The highland soils are often poor, the climate is cooler and rice yields are lower.

In many parts of the world, large numbers of people migrate within a country in search of a better living. In Vietnam, this has not been the case. The reason for this is that the Communist government operated what is known as a 'planned economy'. This is where the development of the country is planned totally by the government. This planning included regulating the numbers of people who were permitted to live in urban and rural areas. Until the 1990s, most Vietnamese people had to apply for a permit even to travel outside their own province.

The slow growth of the industrial sector, and the number of refugees leaving the country also limited urban growth, as did the government's policy of forced resettlement.

People were forced to move from the towns and cities to live in rural areas, especially in the highlands (see page 24).

As a result of these factors, the percentage of the population living in urban areas remained fairly constant – at between 19 and 20 per cent – from the end of the Vietnam War until 1990.

URBANISATION

Since 1990, Vietnam's migration trend has started to become more similar to that of other developing nations, in which waves of migrants leave the countryside and head for the urban centres in search of work and a better standard of living. This is partly due to the opening up of the Vietnamese economy, which has given people an opportunity to work outside the state-controlled industries and services. Together with a change in Vietnam's 1992 constitution, which grants all citizens the right to search for employment anywhere in the country, this has speeded up the process of urbanisation. By 2000, the percentage of the population living in urban areas had risen to 24 per cent.

The rural population density on the Dalat Plateau is high, but much lower than in the river delta areas.

URBAN POPULATION

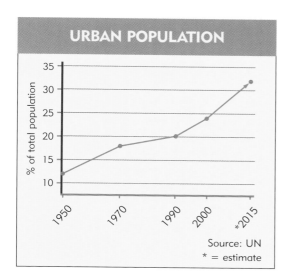

% of total population

Source: UN
* = estimate

ABOVE: The number of motorcycles is increasing rapidly in Hanoi as the economy develops.

THE GROWTH OF HO CHI MINH CITY

Ho Chi Minh City is the most popular destination for migrants within Vietnam. By 1996, the numbers of people migrating to Ho Chi Minh City was in excess of 80,000 each year (compared with 22,000 to the capital, Hanoi). The rapid expansion of Ho Chi Minh City has caused problems, including the creation of slums that now house 1.5 million people. Other cities have also suffered as a result of growth, but not to the same extent.

BELOW: A family living in poor housing in Nha Trang.

POPULATION DENSITY

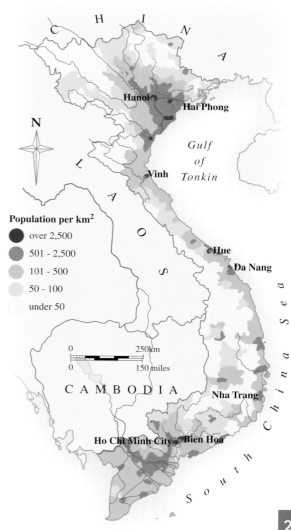

Population per km^2

- over 2,500
- 501 – 2,500
- 101 – 500
- 50 – 100
- under 50

ANCESTRAL TIES

Vietnamese people have a close link to their ancestors and are very strongly attached to the land where their ancestors are buried. Migrants to the cities regularly return to their ancestral lands and indigenous people in the highlands vigorously defend their ancestral land from invading farmers for the same reason.

LANDLESSNESS

A new feature of Vietnamese society is the growing number of landless people. Since the 1980s, the number of landless people in areas such as the Mekong Delta and the Central Highlands has more than doubled as land has started to become privately or state owned. Landless people are now migrating to the big cities in order to find work, which places pressure on the services of Hanoi and Ho Chi Minh City.

Many rural people in northern Vietnam live in extreme poverty.

INTERNATIONAL MIGRATION

International migration in Vietnam over the last 50 years has been almost entirely in one direction – out of the country – because of war and the oppression of the people of the South when the Communists reunified the country.

In the late 1970s and early 1980s, images of desperate people fleeing Vietnam were broadcast on television screens all over the world. Hundreds of thousands of people headed to sea in small boats in the hope of finding refuge in other countries. While many of these so-called 'boat people' were picked up at sea or made it to other countries, thousands lost their lives when their boats sank in storms or they ran out of food.

Vietnamese refugees were often referred to as boat people even when they had left Vietnam by other means. The number who successfully reached asylum between 1975 and 1980 was nearly 840,000. In addition, more than a quarter of a million ethnic Chinese crossed into China by foot in the same period.

A Vietnamese wedding in California, USA, with people wearing a mixture of traditional and Western dress.

WOMEN AND MIGRATION

There are many reasons for women to migrate. Those who become divorced, or run away, or have a baby outside of marriage tend to leave rural areas and head for the cities. Most prefer to go to Ho Chi Minh City: more than 50 per cent of migrants registered in Ho Chi Minh City are female, whereas in Hanoi this figure is only 30 per cent. Ho Chi Minh City has a more tolerant population than Hanoi. There are also more employment opportunities for single women, especially in light industry, such as textiles and garment production, and service industries.

A young woman working in a textile factory in Ho Chi Minh City.

A poor man in Hanoi waits outside a health clinic with his baby.

The country is still recovering from the effects of war and has only recently begun to change from an agricultural-based society towards an urban-based one. With the relaxing of state control over the last 10 years, aspects of Vietnamese life are changing in many ways. There are more individual freedoms: for example, people can now live where they want. People are also living longer than ever before. However, the provision of healthcare and education is declining. Also, a gap is beginning to develop between the rich and poor, and urban and rural populations.

THE BEGINNINGS OF AN UNEQUAL SOCIETY

In Vietnam during the 1970s, the planned economy (see page 28) appeared to be working on a social level. Schools, medical centres and childcare services were established in every village and people were guaranteed minimum food supplies. The elderly and ill were also cared for within the system. However, following the withdrawal of aid by the Soviet Union (see page 45), and with the population growing rapidly, the system began to fail.

Today, although it still adheres to many Communist principals, Vietnam has started to develop its economy along Western lines. The result has been major economic growth but also a widening gap between rich and poor and between regions.

HEALTH

Today, the proportion of people who are under 13 years old is still over 30 per cent but it is getting smaller as people have fewer children and live longer. In 1960, the average life expectancy was just 44 years; today this has risen to 69. Much of this is due to the end of

The modern Benh Vien Hung hospital in Ho Chi Minh City.

UNDER-FIVE MORTALITY RATE

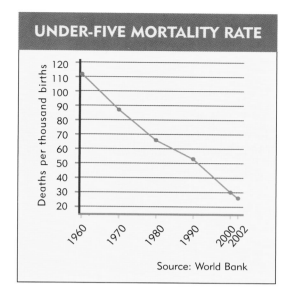

Deaths per thousand births

120, 110, 100, 90, 80, 70, 60, 50, 40, 30, 20

1960, 1970, 1980, 1990, 2000 2002

Source: World Bank

ABOVE: An elderly woman working in a market near the town of Vinh.

LIFE EXPECTANCY AT BIRTH

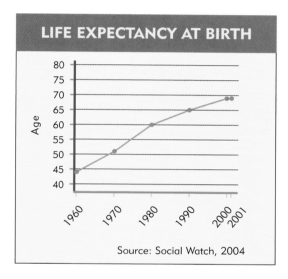

Age

80, 75, 70, 65, 60, 55, 50, 45, 40

1960, 1970, 1980, 1990, 2000 2001

Source: Social Watch, 2004

risen to 69. Much of this is due to the end of the Vietnam War but also to improved diet and better healthcare. Since 1960, the number of children who die before their fifth birthday has also fallen from 112 per thousand to 26 per thousand, but this is still four times higher than in Western countries such as Canada and Germany.

Until recently, healthcare has been widely available under an excellent free system, and access to doctors, nurses and midwives was possible for most villagers and urban dwellers. Recent changes have seen the introduction of fees for healthcare and a system that is no longer available to all. Doctors are now poorly paid and ill-equipped. It is normal for a family member to stay in hospital with an ill relative to provide meals and pay for treatments. A major hospital operation often costs the equivalent of a year's income for a poor family.

Vietnam is still a very poor country, despite the poverty rate falling from 57 per cent in 1992–93 to 38 per cent in 1997–98. A quarter of the population still cannot meet their basic food requirements. Vietnamese people continue to suffer from the effects of the Vietnam War: the toxic chemicals used by the Americans to kill large areas of forest during the war have led to excessive numbers of birth defects.

The growing number of motor vehicles on Vietnam's roads has led to over 7,000 people being killed and 25,000 injured in motor accidents each year.

The Vietnamese government has initiated an immunisation campaign to help prevent diseases such as poliomyelitis and whooping cough. It is also running educational campaigns on improving hygiene and preventing infectious diseases. The government now promotes a longer period of breastfeeding to help cut the incidence of infant malnutrition.

The wreckage of a truck after a serious road accident in northern Vietnam.

Collecting water from a well in a rural area near the city of Nha Trang.

BASIC SERVICES

The provision of basic services to Vietnamese homes, such as clean water, electricity and drainage, is improving slowly. However, there is a large difference in access to these services in rural and urban areas. Rural areas and the poorer areas of the central regions still have to rely on collecting water from a well. In addition, Vietnam has a poorly developed communication network.

TELECOMMUNICATIONS DATA (PER 1,000 PEOPLE)	
Mainline Phones	48
Mobile Phones	23
Internet Users	18

Source: World Bank, 2002

VIETNAMESE DIET

The Vietnamese diet is based around rice, which has been the staple food for thousands of years. Along with rice, the Vietnamese eat a wide variety of vegetables, herbs and fruit including chillies, cabbage, lotus flowers, ginger and lemon.

One of the most important ingredients in almost every dish is a special fish sauce called *nuoc nam*, which is unique to Vietnam. It is made from fermented fish and is the ingredient that gives Vietnamese food its distinctive flavour.

Fish is also a mainstay of the Vietnamese diet. Many types of sea fish are caught in the waters off its coastline, including tuna, ray and shark. The two large river deltas also provide seafood, especially eels and shrimps.

People reading daily newspapers on display in Hanoi (see Media, right).

Every morning, millions of Vietnamese start their day with a steaming bowl of *pho*, a noodle soup that is considered by many nutritionists and cookery experts as one of the best soups in the world. It has a base of meat or fish stock, with garlic, spring onion, rice, slivers of meat, chillies, black pepper and the key Vietnamese ingredient, *nuoc nam* (fish sauce). When the soup is ready to serve, rice noodles are dunked for 5 seconds into boiling water before being slid into the soup.

Many people in cities like Hanoi have their favourite *pho* stall. This is generally a collection of small stoves operated by one or two cooks. Most business people and workers have breakfast on the way to work. *Pho* is the perfect fast food as it is warming and nourishing and can be prepared in very little time.

Pho soup is often cooked at stalls in the street and served for breakfast to people on their way to work.

Meat dishes generally include pork, beef, chicken and snake, although wild meat, including deer and wild pig, is also cooked in more remote areas.

The tropical climate in the lowlands and the temperate climate in the highlands means that many different types of fruit can be cultivated, including bananas, rambutans, apples, mangoes, pineapples and papayas. In addition, tea is grown in the highlands and is the most important national beverage.

MEDIA

Whilst many areas of Vietnamese society are being opened up to Western influence, the media is one area in which the government retains complete control. All television, radio, telephone and Internet services are run by government agencies. The same is true for all newspapers, printing presses and publishing houses. In this way, the Vietnamese government controls virtually all information that is available to the general population. Anyone trying to produce or distribute an unofficial publication,

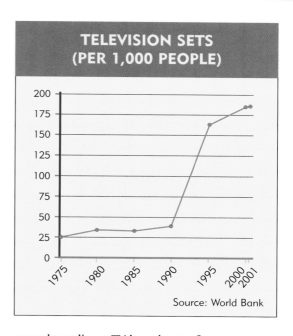

TELEVISION SETS (PER 1,000 PEOPLE)

Source: World Bank

or make radio or TV broadcasts, faces many obstacles and the government is quick to punish anyone whose work is considered anti-government. The control of information, however, is not as easy as it once was because of satellite TV and the Internet.

RELIGION

Religion is an important part of life and the way the Vietnamese perceive the world is often radically different from that of Westerners. An interesting example of this is that when the Vietnamese get old they are generally happy with the increased status they have in society rather than the fact that they are physically declining. Life is also believed to be cyclical, with the soul being reincarnated time after time.

Four great philosophies and religions have shaped the lives of the Vietnamese people over the last 2,000 years: Confucianism, Taoism, Buddhism and Christianity. Over centuries, the religions of Taoism, Buddhism and Confucianism have blended with traditional Chinese beliefs and Vietnamese ancestor worship to form what is known as the 'Triple Religion' or Tam Giao. More than two-thirds of the population consider themselves Buddhists, but when it comes to family or civic duties they are likely to follow Confucianism. Equally when asked about the meaning of life their ideas are generally Taoist. For the many indigenous peoples of Vietnam ancestor worship is an important part of life.

This 14m-high statue of the Buddha overlooks the city of Nha Trang.

EDUCATION

Education has traditionally been held in very high regard in Vietnamese society. Considering the country's economic situation, it has an exceptionally high literacy rate of 94 per cent. Vietnam can also boast that its first national university was founded in 1076. Primary school is compulsory for five years until the age of 11. Only between 30 and 40 per cent continue

A young boy returning from school in Can Tho in southern Vietnam.

beyond primary school education to attend secondary school. Parents are very enthusiastic about getting the best education for their children, not only to help them to get a better job but also because of their Confucian beliefs. In Confucianism, a person's level of academic achievement helps create their personality and status.

Until 1989, Vietnam had remarkably high standards of education throughout the country. During the 1990s, the education system began to decline following the loss of financial support from the Soviet Union (see page 45). Whereas education used to be free for the first 12 years, this has been cut back to just the first three years. Teachers once held highly respected positions in society. Today their salaries are so low that they earn less than factory workers and motorcycle taxi drivers. These changes have led to parents sending children out to work at a much younger age, and teachers often have to find private students to increase their income.

The school day generally runs from 7am to 11.15am and from 1pm to 5pm, but because of the shortage of teachers and space, it is common for children to attend just one of these sessions.

A few of the 12,000 students studying at Dalat University.

THE LUNAR CALENDAR

In many parts of the world, including Europe, the Americas, Australia and New Zealand, people follow what is known as the Gregorian calendar, which is based on the passage of the Earth around the Sun. In Vietnam and some other countries, such as China, people use the lunar calendar, based on the Moon's movements around the Earth.

Each lunar month has 29 or 30 days, which results in years with 355 days. Approximately every third year is a leap year, when an extra month is added between the third and fourth months to keep the lunar year synchronised with the solar year.

Year one of the Vietnamese lunar calendar corresponds to 2637 BC. Instead of dividing the time into centuries, the Vietnamese calendar divides it into periods of 60 years, called *hoi*. Each *hoi* is divided into two cycles, one of six units of 10 years and the other of five units of 12 years, which run simultaneously.

Each lunar year is associated with an animal. 2005 is the year of the rooster, 2006 is the dog and 2007 is the pig.

FAMILY LIFE

As in many other Asian countries, life for most Vietnamese revolves around the family. It is usual for grandparents, parents and children to live together. In contrast to many Western societies, age is highly respected in Vietnamese society.

Children are expected to work hard from an early age. Boys and girls cook and clean the house, and also care for younger brothers and sisters when their mother is out at work. The eldest son is also responsible for making sure his brothers and sisters behave well. Eventually, the eldest son will be responsible for the whole family, looking after his parents in old age and caring for the shrines of his ancestors.

The family in Vietnam is a strong unit and it has played an important part in helping people to survive the terrible effects of war. Within Vietnamese families, those who are better off financially or in good health have an obligation to help others who are less fortunate.

ROLES OF WOMEN

There have been many changes in the way women are treated within society. Vietnamese women are used to working, especially as

A woman salt worker takes a break, near the town of Tuy Hoa.

during the many wars women have had to run the home, tend the fields and take on additional work to support the family. The Communist government recognised and strengthened women's position in society and it is not unusual to see women in positions of power in the government. Women are also represented by the Women's Union, which was established in 1930 and still has considerable influence.

ABOVE: Mealtimes often involve the whole family sitting down to eat together.

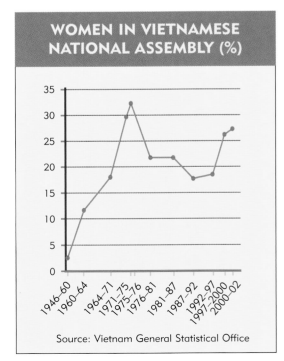

WOMEN IN VIETNAMESE NATIONAL ASSEMBLY (%)

Source: Vietnam General Statistical Office

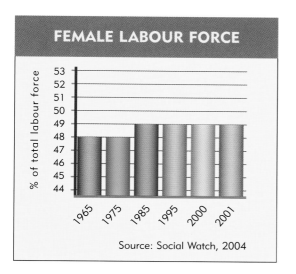

FEMALE LABOUR FORCE

% of total labour force

53
52
51
50
49
48
47
46
45
44

1965 · 1975 · 1985 · 1995 · 2000 · 2001

Source: Social Watch, 2004

ABOVE: Each morning people exercise in the parks in Hanoi.

However, in many areas of Vietnamese life, great inequality still exists. For example, since 1975 the numbers of women in important government jobs has declined sharply. Also, male children are seen as very important in traditional Vietnamese life as they will carry forward the family line and continue the worship of the ancestors.

RECREATION

Every day, early in the morning, in cities like Hanoi thousands of people head for the parks and open areas to exercise. Jogging, Tai Chi (a form of martial art), stretching and playing games such as badminton, are all part of the exercise regime of millions of Vietnamese.

Football is the country's top spectator sport. In the scorching Vietnamese summer, water parks are also extremely popular, as are the many beaches along the coast. During the year there are many religious and cultural festivals throughout Vietnam. The most important of these is known as the Tet (see case study).

CASE STUDY
THE TET

The Tet Nguyen Dan festival is the most important day of the Vietnamese calendar and marks the beginning of a new lunar year (see page 37). The festival falls between 19 January and 20 February each year.

The Tet, as it is known, is much more than a simple New Year celebration: it is a colourful festival lasting for about two weeks. It is a time when families gather, when all accounts are settled and any grudges forgotten. It is also a time for feasting and remembering the ancestors. Money and presents also flood in from relatives living abroad. Workers often receive an extra month's wages prior to the Tet to help pay for the family parties.

Children enjoying themselves at a water park in Ho Chi Minh City.

Rice being planted out in paddies near Sapa. Rice is the most important food crop in Vietnam.

Vietnam is one of the poorest countries in Asia. Among the reasons for the country's poor economic performance are the devastating wars it has suffered, and the loss of financial support from the former Soviet Union (see page 45). However, since 1986, Vietnam has made substantial progress in developing its economy.

Today Vietnam's economy can be divided into three main sections – agriculture, industry and services. Agricultural and industrial production includes the parts of the economy where products are cultivated, mined or manufactured. Services are the activities that are paid for although no actual goods are produced, such as tourism or banking.

AGRICULTURE

The economy is still largely based on agriculture and millions of workers throughout the country are involved in producing crops such as rice, sugar, cashew nuts, bananas and rubber. Agriculture is heavily dependent on human labour and only in the intensively farmed areas of the Mekong and Red River deltas is much use made of machinery. Until the mid-1980s, Vietnam produced food crops mainly on a subsistence basis to feed its own population. Since 1986, agricultural production has increased steadily and, having once been an importer of rice, Vietnam is now the world's second-largest exporter.

Rice is the staple food of most Vietnamese people, supplemented by corn, maize, cassava and sweet potato. Between 1995 and 2002, the planted area of rice rose from 53,398,000 hectares to 69,194,000 hectares. More importantly, the production of cereals grew from 330.9kg per capita to 396.4kg per capita,

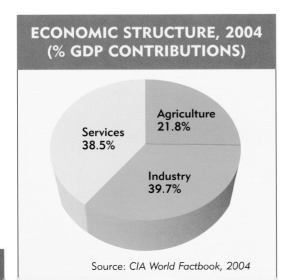

ECONOMIC STRUCTURE, 2004 (% GDP CONTRIBUTIONS)

Services 38.5%

Agriculture 21.8%

Industry 39.7%

Source: *CIA World Factbook, 2004*

RICE PRODUCTION, 1995–2002

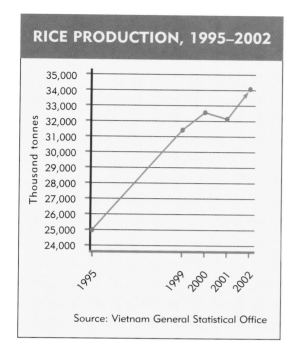

Source: Vietnam General Statistical Office

Buffalo are still widely used in agriculture in the northern half of Vietnam.

LIVESTOCK

Vietnam's agricultural system uses mainly human labour. There is little waste and by-products of crop production are used to feed livestock or as organic fertiliser on the fields. Between 1995 and 2002, buffalo and cattle numbers remained fairly stable at 2.9 million and 4.1 million respectively. However, over the same period, the number of pigs being reared rose from 16.3 million to 23.2 million. Other animals raised include, goats, chickens and even snakes in special snake farms.

which helped the country to feed its rapidly growing population. Rice is the main agricultural crop of Vietnam but the production of cash crops for use by local industries or for export has grown rapidly since the mid-1980s. These cash crops include sugar cane, coffee, soybean, cotton and tobacco.

The production of coffee has grown rapidly from 207,000 tons in 1995 to 758,000 tons in 2002. Sugar cane production rose from 107,111,000 tons to 168,235,000 tons between 1997 and 2002, and soybean production increased from 1,255,000 tons to 2,014,000 tons in the same period.

In contrast to many other developing nations, Vietnam's agricultural production is still growing rapidly. One reason for this is that the state-controlled agriculture under Communism was highly inefficient, so when the economy began to develop in the 1980s and 1990s it did so from a very low base. Consequently, the growth figures since then have been very high. Today, the agricultural sector still accounts for just under 22 per cent of Vietnam's GDP (gross domestic product) and employs 35 per cent of the workforce.

AGRICULTURE

Buffalo
Cattle
Rice
Tea and Coffee
Soybean
Tobacco
Cotton
Jute
Sugar (grown along coast between Red and Mekong deltas)

FISHING

The seas and waterways of Vietnam provide the majority of the country's dietary protein as well as many valuable export commodities. Vietnam has a long coastline with a broad continental shelf jutting out into the South China Sea. The shallow waters above the continental shelf provide abundant fishing grounds for thousands of Vietnamese fishermen. This part of the economy has been growing rapidly, and in the period between 1990 and 2002 the fish catch more than doubled from 728,500 tons to 1,797,100 tons. The total value of Vietnam's marine fishery is about US$1 billion and constitutes one of the most important sources of foreign income. However, it is taking inshore fishermen much more time and effort than before to land the same size catch, which indicates that fish stocks are being depleted by overfishing.

Dozens of fishing boats and houseboats moored in Cat Ba Harbour, north-east Vietnam.

Consequently, the fish catch is predicted to fall during the 10 years from 2005 to 2015.

The production of fish from fish farms has increased more than four times from 162,100 tons in 1990 to 781,400 tons in 2002. Large areas of coastal mangrove swamp have been converted into shrimp farms, and more than half of all farmed fish are produced in the Mekong Delta.

Farmed shrimps for sale in Cholon Market, Ho Chi Minh City.

Felled timber being loaded on to a truck near Bien Hoa.

FORESTRY

Forest resources are very important to the population because millions of people rely on wood for cooking and heating (see pages 18–19), and hundreds of thousands of people rely on timber and other forest products for employment. Apart from wood, the forests provide valuable products such as rattan for furniture-making and bamboo for scaffolding. Also, more than a thousand medicinal plants, mainly from forests, are used in traditional medicine.

Unlike other parts of the economy, timber production fell from 34,455,000m^3 in 1990 to 24,281,000m^3 in 2002. The Vietnamese government initiated a planting programme and, over the same period, the area of planted production forest almost doubled from 100,300 hectares to 191,820 hectares.

CASE STUDY
FURNITURE MAKING

Vietnam has a number of factories making garden furniture, which is sold throughout the world. The raw materials used come from both local forests and timber imported from other South-east Asian countries.

The factories, based mainly near Ho Chi Minh City, have two main seasonal peaks of activity. The first is to supply furniture to European shops in time for their early summer in May and June, when most garden furniture is sold. The second is to cater for the high sales in Australia and New Zealand at the beginning of their summer in December to January.

Many of the processes in the factories are carried out manually. Assembling, sanding and putting protective oil on the finished furniture are all done by hand.

A furniture factory in Bien Hoa making goods for export.

A woman collecting latex from rubber trees in a plantation in the Mekong Delta.

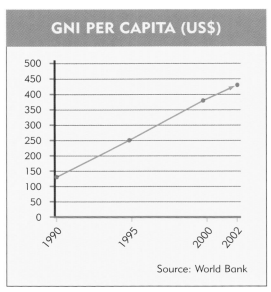

Source: World Bank

INDUSTRY

MANUFACTURING

The manufacturing sector is not as important as agriculture to the Vietnamese economy but it is growing rapidly. Most of the country's industry and infrastructure, such as roads and ports, was almost completely destroyed during the Vietnam War. In the first decade after the war, emphasis was given to the rebuilding of roads, bridges and power systems, along with the traditional industries of mining and the processing of agricultural produce. During the late 1980s and early 1990s, Vietnam's economy was one of the fastest growing in South-east Asia, averaging growth of over 8 per cent between 1992 and 1997.

Vietnam's main industries are food processing, garments, shoes, machine building, mining, cement, chemical fertiliser, glass, tyres, oil, coal, steel and paper. The fastest growing parts of the manufacturing sector are those involving skilled manual labour, such as the production of fashion clothing and electrical goods including computers and mobile phones. Because wages are low, Vietnam can produce goods such as clothing and textiles at very competitive prices.

MAJOR TRADING PARTNERS (% OF VALUE), 2002

EXPORTS

IMPORTS

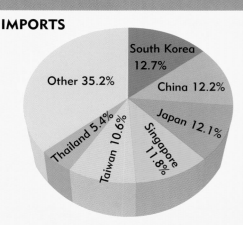

Source: CIA World Factbook, 2003

CASE STUDY
VIETNAMESE CLOTHING FOR THE WEALTHY

Workers in a garment factory in Ho Chi Minh City making fur-lined jackets for export to Europe.

Tens of thousands of Vietnamese workers are employed in the garment-making industries. Many of these people work for very low wages, equivalent to just US$2–3 a day, making items such as shirts, underwear and, more recently, sportswear. Many Vietnamese work in very poor conditions and are badly paid. They often have to work long hours and have little job security. It is common for people to work 14 hours a day for 6 or 7 days a week during the peak export season in the second half of the year. Once the orders are completed, however, the workers often have no job or income for months.

The system of cheap labour working in very poor conditions is doubly unjust because many of the items made in Vietnam are fashion clothing and sportswear that are sold in Western countries for very high prices.

EXPORTS AND TRADE

For many years up until the 1980s, the economy of Vietnam was largely supported by the former Soviet Union. As a consequence, most trade was almost entirely with other Communist countries. Vietnam traded crude oil, wood and sugar cane for refined oil, machinery and weapons. As the value of Vietnam's exported raw products was less than that of the imported manufactured goods, the Soviet Union's aid amounted to the equivalent of half the country's GDP. When the whole Soviet system collapsed in 1991, the Vietnamese government suddenly had to establish trade links with other countries. Almost overnight Vietnam started trading with China, Hong Kong, Singapore, South Korea, Thailand and a number of Western nations.

Although many sectors of the Vietnamese economy are developing rapidly, some manufactured goods are still of poor quality and bring in little export income. However, the agricultural sector is strong and earns substantial foreign income. Of all Vietnam's natural resources, oil is the most important, accounting for 22 per cent of all exports in 2002.

Boats carrying scrap metal in the busy port of Hai Phong.

45

THE SERVICE INDUSTRIES

The growth of the service sector is tied to Vietnam's economic development. The economy has only recently started to develop rapidly and it is still largely agriculture-based. However, under Communism the country had excellent services, such as health and education, which employed many people. Large numbers of the working population were also employed in administration. Today the number of government jobs has fallen sharply but many new service jobs have been created in areas such as hotels, tourism and banking.

The service sector accounts for only 38.5 per cent of the country's GDP. This compares with countries such as Canada where services account for 71.2 per cent of GDP and India where services account for 50 per cent. This sector of the economy is likely to grow rapidly in the next decade, partly because of the increasing numbers of tourists visiting the country. The rugged north-west of the country attracts millions of visitors who come to see the many indigenous groups and the beautiful landscapes in which they live. Other major tourist destinations include Hanoi, Da Nang, Hue, Nha Trang, Ha Long Bay, Dalat, Ho Chi Minh City and the Mekong Delta.

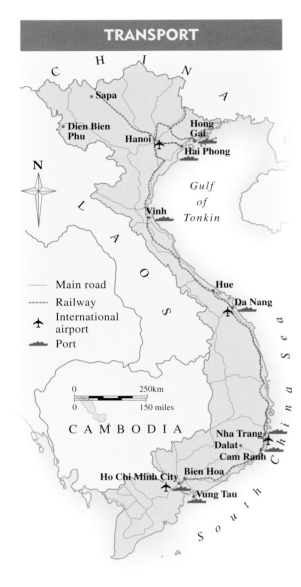

TRANSPORT

— Main road
┈┈┈ Railway
✈ International airport
⚓ Port

European tourists on a cruise around Ha Long Bay.

TRANSPORT AND COMMUNICATIONS

Vietnam has a reasonable network of roads and railways linking the country's main economic areas. In 2002, Vietnam had 93,300km of roads of which 22,418km were paved and 68,882km were unpaved or dirt roads. However, this network is mainly restricted to the lowland areas, which occupy just a quarter of the country but contain more than 80 per cent of the population. The rugged mountainous areas, which occupy the other three-quarters of the country, are poorly served by roads and have almost no railways.

Vietnam is a maritime nation with a long coastline and access to one of the busiest shipping areas in Asia. The country has numerous harbours and ports, which support large fishing fleets and are the main gateways for imports and exports. The main ports and harbours are Cam Ranh, Da Nang, Hai Phong, Ho Chi Minh City, Hong Gai, Nha Trang, Vinh

Heavy traffic in Ho Chi Minh City, with cyclists wearing masks to protect them from the pollution.

and Vung Tau. Vietnam also has a network of 47 airports of which 24 have paved runways. The main international airports are in Hanoi and Ho Chi Minh City, though cities like Da Nang and Nha Trang are developing their airports in order to accommodate the increasing numbers of foreign tourists.

TOURISM IN SAPA

Sapa is a small hill town close to the Chinese border in north-west Vietnam, set in a spectacular mountain landscape with dramatic rice terraces. It is one of the main market towns for a number of Vietnam's indigenous peoples, including the Black Hmong and the Thai. Despite being in a remote and poor area of the country, Sapa has become one of Vietnam's main tourist attractions. Apart from the breathtaking scenery, tourists flock to the markets where it is possible to buy handicrafts made by local people. The main products are beautifully woven textiles made from hemp and died with indigo and other natural plant dyes.

A tourist in Sapa buying textiles from Hmong and Dao women.

Tourism in and around Sapa has boosted the local economy, and the income it generates is being used to improve the lives of the hill people by providing schools and health facilities.

Endangered spotted deer in the Cuc Phuong National Park.

Vietnam is a large and environmentally diverse country with many different types of natural environments. There are four main ecological areas: the northern highlands, the Mekong and Red River deltas, the central mountain chain and the coastal plain. Vietnam is facing a number of environmental problems. Of these, deforestation is the most serious but hunting, air pollution, water pollution and overfishing of marine fish are all causes for concern.

BIODIVERSITY

Vietnam has an extremely high biodiversity for a country of its size. In part this is because Vietnam contains a wide variety of habitats.

The job of listing all the species that occur in the country is still incomplete, but in the steep jungle slopes of the Truong Son mountain range alone, six new mammal species were discovered in the 10 years since 1995. This is more than in the rest of the world in the 100 years since 1905. Some of the rarest animals include the kouprey (a wild ox), the Asian elephant, the tiger, the Javan rhino, the green

VIETNAM'S BIODIVERSITY IN FIGURES

	NUMBER OF SPECIES
Higher plants	12,000+
Insects	5,000+
Mammals	273
Birds	773
Reptiles	180
Amphibians	80

Source: IUCN (International Union for the Conservation of Nature); UNEP

peacock and the saola, a species of antelope that was only discovered in 1996.

In recent decades – and especially since the border between China and Vietnam was reopened – the country's biodiversity has become seriously threatened. Deforestation and the over-exploitation of plant and animal species for commercial purposes are the two main causes.

FOREST HABITATS

In the north of the country, the Hoang Lien mountains and the limestone ranges of the Guangxi mountains are biologically similar to southern China. The hill forests comprise both evergreen and semi-evergreen tree species. The montane forests change with altitude from oaks and chestnuts mixed with conifers to upper montane forests dominated by conifers with an under-storey of bamboo. These remote forests provide the habitat for many rare and endangered species.

The Truong Son mountain range running along the spine of the country is biologically distinct from the northern mountain ranges, and contains many species that are found only in Vietnam.

The highland forests are rich in insect species such as butterflies.

COASTAL ENVIRONMENTS

Vietnam has a long coastline with thousands of small islands off the coast. Cold currents sweep south in winter and warm currents flow north in summer, bringing with them nutrient-rich sea water that supports rich aquatic life. The Vietnamese fishery areas contain many commercial species (see page 20).

More than 295 species of coral have been recorded in Vietnamese waters but many of these are now threatened. Threats include siltation from land, overfishing of fish and invertebrates such as shrimps, the use of explosives for fishing and the collection of items for the souvenir trade. Coral is also mined and mixed with cement and used in construction. Mining coral is illegal but the practice continues because the law is not enforced.

The development of eco-tourism along the coast is providing the opportunity for foreign visitors to scuba dive to see the reef life without damaging the environment. Apart from the soft and hard corals and the smaller reef fish, it is also possible to see grey nurse sharks and nurse sharks.

In parts of southern Vietnam, coastal mangrove forests have been destroyed to make way for shrimp farms like this one.

A view of the tropical waters of the South China Sea and a coastal island near Nha Trang.

THE MEKONG DELTA

The Mekong Delta occupies 12 per cent of the country, contains 20 per cent of the population and produces 60 per cent of the country's food crops. Despite this, the Mekong

TOURISM AND TURTLES

Many of the prime areas for developing tourism in Vietnam, where beautiful tropical seas lap on to golden sandy beaches, are also ideal egg-laying locations for rare species of turtle. Five turtle species are found in the South China Sea, including hawksbill, green and loggerhead turtles. All five are recognised as globally threatened.

Recent research has shown that some turtle nesting occurs in north-east Vietnam, but the small islands off the coast probably provide the best nesting areas. However, tourist development on the islands in Ha Long Bay and near Nha Trang could disturb the turtles' nesting sites and make the turtles less likely to breed.

A rare hawksbill turtle laying its eggs on a tropical beach.

Delta is still extremely important as a breeding area for many ocean-going fish and crustaceans such as crabs and shrimps. It is also an important wetland habitat and a stopover for migrating birds such as the red-necked crane.

In the southern parts of the delta, there are estuarine crocodiles that can weigh over a tonne, and numerous snake species inhabit the swamps and feed on frogs, birds and eggs. The Vietnamese enjoy eating snake meat and, because of this, some species are now being overhunted.

One of the environmental challenges facing people in the Mekong Delta is how to keep the river channels clean. For centuries, the usual way of disposing of sewage and garbage was to throw it into the river. As the population increases, this practice is starting to cause serious pollution.

A boat on one of the many channels of the Mekong Delta.

RURAL PROBLEMS
DEFORESTATION

Originally Vietnam was almost completely covered in forest, from great mangrove forests in the deltas to dense rainforest in the uplands. Today, deforestation is considered by many experts to be the single most serious environmental problem facing Vietnam. In 1943, forest covered about 45 per cent of the entire country but this had fallen to less than 30 per cent by 1998. The worst affected areas are mountain areas in the Central Highlands. Not only have large areas of forest been lost but the quality of much of the remaining forest has been degraded so that the species diversity is much lower than in natural forests.

There are many causes of deforestation. Vietnam's population has grown rapidly since 1975 and many areas of forest have been cleared for new settlements, as well as for the cultivation of cash crops such as rubber. In addition, the use of natural forest for firewood, illegal logging and the lasting effects of the millions of litres of chemical defoliants used in the Vietnam War have all contributed to Vietnam's forest loss.

Forest loss is a severe problem because it affects biodiversity, causes the loss of valuable timber and leads to a higher incidence of flash floods and droughts. In response, the government has organised a national plan to reafforest 5 million hectares.

ABOVE: Deforestation is becoming a major problem in the Central Highlands near Dalat.

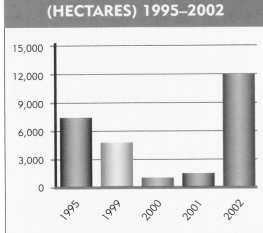

FOREST DESTRUCTION, (HECTARES) 1995–2002

Source: Vietnam General Statistical Office

Soil erosion caused by deforestation of steep mountainsides near Dalat.

LAND DEGRADATION

For a country like Vietnam, whose economy is largely based on agriculture, land degradation poses a major threat to both biodiversity and human health. In the lowlands, the construction of roads, industrial sites and refuse dumps is leading to a loss of rice-growing areas. However, the situation is much more serious in the highlands that cover 75 per cent of the country. Here, poor agricultural techniques are causing serious soil erosion. In the worst affected areas, soil is being lost from the steep slopes at a rate of between 60 and 200 tonnes per hectare per year. This soil loss causes problems for agriculture locally, and leads to the silting up of many waterways, which reduces the generating life of many HEP stations (see pages 18–19).

CASE STUDY
CHEMICALS AND VEGETABLES

Many of the workers growing perennial cash crops, such as bananas, rubber, tea and coffee, are employed to spray herbicides and pesticides on the plants throughout the year. In the case of bananas, this can involve as many as 40 applications of what are often toxic chemicals. In addition to the damage to native wildlife, especially insects and the birds that feed on them, the workers themselves are exposed to high levels of poisonous chemicals. Many workers fall ill and their children can be affected by birth defects caused by the chemicals.

A young man spraying rubber tree seedlings with pesticide near Bien Hoa.

Contamination of waterways with human sewage and rubbish is a problem in big cities such as Nha Trang.

CHINA

Ba Be National Park

Cat Ba National Park

Ba Vi National Park

Cuc Phuong National Park

Gulf of Tonkin

N

LAOS

Ben En National Park

Bach Ma National Park

0   250km
0   150 miles

CAMBODIA

Yok Don National Park

Tam Nong National Park

Cat Tien National Park

U Minh National Park

Con Dao National Park

South China Sea

URBAN PROBLEMS
WASTE MANAGEMENT

In the last 15 years Vietnam has undergone a dramatic change in the way its urban population consumes resources and disposes of waste. A little over a decade ago, most Vietnamese people consumed little in the way of resources that were not organic. Most of the waste generated was organic too and much of it could be fed to animals or used as fertiliser. Plastics and metal were recycled. As the Vietnamese economy has become more industrialised, problems with waste management have increased. The change from a low-consumption society towards a 'one-use, throw-away' one is causing major environmental problems. In Ho Chi Minh City, for example, the Dong Thanh landfill site was receiving between 100 and 200 tons of waste per day in 1995. In 2004, the site received more than 4,000 tons (equivalent to 600–700 truckloads) of waste, resulting in contamination of local water supplies and other environmental problems.

POLLUTION

Vietnam's increased industrial pollution stems from two main causes. The first is that many of the established industries use old technology and have little regulation of their waste output. The second is the waste generated by the new industries that are developing as the country's economy develops. The priority for economic growth has led to serious pollution in many of Vietnam's industrial areas. While government regulations do exist, they are rarely enforced.

Vietnamese cities such as the capital Hanoi and Ho Chi Minh City are unusual in that, despite being cities with populations of more

Many people wear facemasks in cities to protect themselves against air pollution.

than 2 million and 5 million respectively, air pollution is a relatively new problem. Air pollution did exist in the 1980s but it was largely restricted to the areas around large industrial plants, such as iron smelters and power stations. At the same time, however, the streets of these cities were typically full of non-polluting bicycles, scooters and the occasional smoky truck.

This began to change in the early 1990s, when the number of motorcycles overtook the number of bicycles. Motorised vehicles are now the main source of atmospheric pollution in urban areas. Every year, the levels of carbon monoxide, sulphur dioxide and nitrous oxides increase as more vehicles take to the roads.

PROTECTED AREAS

In response to some of the environmental threats outlined above, Vietnamese governments over the last 20 years have established a network of national parks and other protected areas in order to safeguard the habitats of many rare species. There are also new laws to try and prevent trade in endangered wildlife.

The first national park, Cuc Phuong, was established in 1962. Almost all of the other protected areas were established in 1986 and now cover 1.1 million hectares or 3 per cent of the country's surface area. However, the Ministry of Forestry has only 10,000 forest guards, which makes policing the protected areas very difficult.

CASE STUDY
ENDANGERED PRIMATE RESCUE

One of a number of positive projects being undertaken in Vietnam is the Endangered Primate Rescue Centre in Cuc Phuong National Park. The aim is to provide a safe place for injured monkeys – and monkeys confiscated from people who kept them as pets – to recover before being released back into the wild. However, some have been pets for too long to be freed, and others do not have suitable safe habitats in which to be released. The centre cares for about 80 primates at a time, including langurs, gibbons and loris. Some of the rarest monkeys are bred at the centre, while others provide scientists with a rare opportunity to study them at close quarters.

A rare langur with a keeper at the Endangered Primate Rescue Centre.

Making garden furniture for export in a modern factory near Bien Hoa.

Vietnam occupies a strategic position in the world. It shares a border with China, which will soon be the world's largest economy. There will be increasing demand from its powerful neighbour for raw materials and goods, which will help Vietnam's economy to grow in the first half of the twenty-first century. It is also close to the 'tiger' economies of South-east Asia, such as Thailand and Taiwan.

A young man shows off his wealth with a new moped and a suit.

Vietnam has immense natural wealth. It is rich in commodities that are in demand in South-east Asia and throughout the world. For example, the country has major reserves of oil, gas and coal which gives it a significant advantage over many other developing nations that have to import expensive fossil fuels. The country also has the advantage of climatic and geographical conditions that are suitable for growing huge quantities of rice to feed its population.

GROWING INEQUALITY

From the 1950s onwards, Vietnam's Communist government tried to create equal development in all parts of the country. Until the 1990s, this policy was successful, and wealth was evenly distributed between urban and rural dwellers and between regions. For example, each village had a health centre and a school, and the elderly and the sick were cared for by the state. Today, however, there is a growing gap between different parts of society. Schooling and healthcare are no longer free to all, which disadvantages the poorer members of society. Furthermore, foreign investment in industry is creating better-paid jobs in the cities, which are attracting migrants from the countryside.

The increasing industrialisation of agriculture is also having an effect on Vietnamese society. Many of the people who have been resettled in the highlands have been sent there to work on new agricultural projects growing cash crops such as coffee. Much of the land that has been taken over for these projects was formerly the traditional land of minority ethnic groups, and this has led to unrest in some areas. Also, as land is no longer owned communally in all parts of the country, the number of landless people is rising alarmingly. The percentage of people living in the Mekong Delta who are landless rose from 14.6 per cent in 1992 to 37.6 per cent in 2000.

Inequality is one of the most serious issues that Vietnam has to address as its economy develops. The country is unusual for a developing nation in that parts of its education and healthcare systems are actually getting worse. However, the gap between rich and poor has not reached the levels found in some countries, such as Mexico and Brazil.

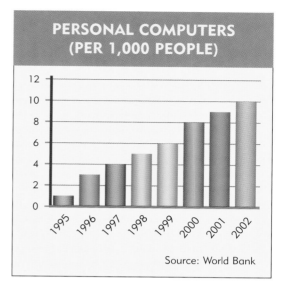

PERSONAL COMPUTERS (PER 1,000 PEOPLE)

Source: World Bank

A BRIGHT FUTURE?

With its abundant natural resources (many of which have not yet begun to be exploited), the new industries that are beginning to develop, and the country's young, hard-working population, Vietnam has enormous potential. Its rate of economic growth is already among the fastest in South-east Asia. If it can overcome the problems of social inequality and can develop economically without having a severe impact on the environment, Vietnam's future looks very promising.

The house of a poor Hmong family near Sapa.

Agent Orange A mixture of chemicals used by the American military during the Vietnam War to kill large areas of forest.

Arid A term used to describe an environment with an annual rainfall that is below 250–300mm per year.

Autonomous Having self government.

Biodiversity The variation (diversity) of biological life within an area.

Biomass fuel Any natural product that can be burnt as fuel, such as wood, rice husks and animal dung.

Catchment area The area over which rainfall is collected.

Colony A country that is occupied and ruled by another foreign country.

Communism A political idea in which all property is owned by the state and where people are paid what they need to survive.

Continental shelf The shallow area of sea close to the coast.

Defoliant A chemical that kills trees by causing the leaves to drop.

Deforestation The clearance of trees, for either timber or land.

Delta The triangular shape formed by a river dividing into a number of channels at its mouth.

Ecosystem A system that represents the relationships within a community of living things and between this community and their non-living environment. An ecosystem can be as small as a pond or as large as the Earth.

Eco-tourism Tourism that is sensitive to its impact on environments and local populations.

Erosion The removal of soil and rock by natural processes, such as wind and rain, or by people, such as through deforestation.

Evaporation To turn from liquid into vapour.

Forced resettlement The moving of people from one area to another whether they want to move or not.

Fossil fuels Fuels such as coal, oil and gas that are made up of the fossilised remains of plants.

GDP (Gross Domestic Product) The monetary value of goods and services produced by a country in a single year.

GNI (Gross National Income) The monetary value of goods and services produced by a country plus any earnings from overseas in a single year. It used to be called Gross National Product (GNP).

Guerillas Small group of independently acting fighters.

Habitat The natural home of a living thing.

HEP (hydroelectric power) Electricity generated using the power of moving water.

Hydrocarbons Substances containing both carbon and hydrogen. Oil is a hydrocarbon.

Infrastructure The basic economic foundations of a country such as roads, bridges, communication systems and proper sewage systems.

Irrigated Farmland supplied with water by an artificial system.

There are many statues of Ho Chi Minh throughout Vietnam like this one in My Tho.

CHỦ TỊCH

Life expectancy The expected number of years a person will live.

Malnourished Suffering from lack of nutrition due to lack of food or poor nutrition.

Migration Moving from one area or country to another.

Monsoon A wind carrying moisture blowing throughout East Asia.

Multiethnic society A society that comprises many ethnic or indigenous groups in a single population.

Plateau (plural plateaux) A high flat area of land.

Pro-birth campaign A campaign encouraging people to have more children.

Production The part of a nation's economy where products are manufactured, mined or cultivated.

Rainforest Dense tropical forest with high rainfall.

Services Economic activities which are paid for although nothing is produced, such as tourism or banking.

Staple The basic food in any given diet.

Temperate climate A climate characterised by mild weather.

Toxic chemicals Chemicals that are poisonous to living organisms.

Tropical climate A climate of constant high temperatures and rainfall found between the Tropics of Cancer and Capricorn.

FURTHER INFORMATION

BOOKS TO READ:
NON FICTION:
Economically Developing Countries: Vietnam by Ole Steen Hansen (Hodder Wayland, 2001) Illustrated reference for KS2–3.

Lonely Planet Guides: Vietnam by Nick Ray and Wendy Yanagihara (Lonely Planet Publications, 2005) A guide for travellers of all ages.

Nations of the World, Vietnam by Jen Green (Raintree, 2003) Illustrated reference for in-depth study with links to KS3–4.

Vietnam Handbook by John Colet (Footprint Handbooks, 2004) A well-written travel guide with lots of background information about the country.

Vietnam Now – A Reporter Returns by David Lamb (Public Affairs, 2002) Looks at Vietnam today through the eyes of a reporter who experienced the country during the height of the Vietnam War.

Catfish and Mandala: A Two-wheeled Voyage through the Landscape and Memory of Vietnam by Andrew Pham (Picador, 2000) This is the story of a slow bicycle tour of Vietnam and other countries of the Pacific Rim by a young Vietnamese American.

Lonely Planet World Food: Vietnam by Richard Sterling and Tinh-My Hoang (Lonely Planet Publications, 2000) A guide to Vietnamese food.

FICTION:
The Quiet American by Graham Greene (first published 1954; widely available in paperback) A classic book about a young, idealistic American living in Vietnam during the last few years of French colonial rule.

WEBSITES:
GENERAL INFORMATION:
CIA World Factbook
www.cia.gov/cia/publications/factbook/geos/vm.html
The US Central Intelligence Agency's online factbook, with statistics and assessments of all countries of the world.

DEVELOPMENT INFORMATION:
United Nations Development Programme (UNDP)
www.undp.org.vn/ehome.htm

United Nations Childrens Fund (UNICEF)
www.unicef.org

WILDLIFE INFORMATION:
World Wildlife Fund – Vietnam
www.wwfindochina.org/

TOURIST INFORMATION:
Vietnam National Administration of Tourism
www.vietnamtourism.com
The Vietnam government's official tourism website.

A view of one of the main channels of the Mekong Delta near My Tho.